Let's Pray!

Heather Reid

Let's Pray!

Prayers for the Elementary Classroom

NOVALIS

© 2007 Novalis, Saint Paul University, Ottawa, Canada

Illustrations: Kari Lehr
Layout: Christiane Lemire

Business Offices:
Novalis Publishing Inc.   Novalis Publishing Inc.
10 Lower Spadina Avenue, Suite 400   4475 Frontenac Street
Toronto, Ontario, Canada   Montréal, Québec, Canada
M5V 2Z2   H2H 2S2

Phone: 1-800-387-7164
Fax: 1-800-204-4140
E-mail: books@novalis.ca
www.novalis.ca

Library and Archives Canada Cataloguing in Publication

Reid, Heather
    Let's pray! : prayers for the elementary classroom / Heather Reid.

ISBN-13: 978-2-89507-845-9
ISBN-10: 2-89507-845-6

    1. Catholic schools–Prayers. 2. Students–Prayer books and
devotions–English. I. Title.

BV283.S3R45 2006   242'.62   C2006-905359-6

Printed in Canada.

We acknowledge the financial support of the Government of Canada through the Book Publishing Industry
Development Program (BPIDP) for our publishing activities.

5   4   3   2   1   10   09   08   07   06

Contents

7   Preface

9   **Part 1: How to Pray with Children**

19   **Part 2: Prayers**

20   For September to June

59   For Times of Sadness

64   For Joyful Times

67   For School Life

75   **Part 3: Prayers of the Christian Tradition**

83   Appendix 1: The Liturgical Year

84   Appendix 2: Other Helpful Resources

85   Appendix 3: Music Resources

Dedicated to the memory of Msgr. Paul Baxter, and to all the students of Monsignor Paul Baxter School, Nepean, Ontario.

Preface

Dear Colleagues,

I'm delighted that you are reading this section, because we as teachers do not always read the introductions in teacher's manuals! If you are reading this, then you are wondering about how to pray with your students. *Part I: How to Pray with Children* answers many of your questions about the "how" of praying with children in the classroom. You will also find out about many things to try and do when teaching your students to pray. *Part 2: Prayers for the Classroom* offers a selection of prayers to get you started.

Praying with children isn't as daunting a task as it may appear, because children teach us if we let them. They do not have our preoccupations with correct form or language. Children relate to God from their hearts in a relaxed, intimate way. We may be surprised to discover our own faith being nurtured as we pray with them.

As their teachers, we can guide them and offer them the opportunity and environment to nurture their prayer. We can allow them the time and freedom to pray during the school day. We can model for them the open stance and comfort of prayer during happy and joyful times. Prayer is not something we can approach in a mechanical, contrived or insincere way.

I have marvelled to listen to the prayers of my students each day: from praying for a classmate's fish to asking God to care for a mom with breast cancer; from thanking God for baby animals in spring, for food and homes, and asking for understanding when parents are divorcing.

As much as we feel driven by the mandated curriculum, including the religious education programs we use, praying with children is one of the primary ways to help them grow in faith.

When we provide opportunities for group prayer – and, indeed, in a way teach children to pray – we give them a lifelong gift!

Heather Reid

Part 1
How to Pray with Children

elcome to a user-friendly book about how to pray with primary and junior students. You will find here many prayers for every day – the liturgical year, the school year, and especially all those happy and sad times that every school goes through. Part 1 will answer most of your questions and help you prepare to pray with the children in your classroom.

These prayers are not meant to replace the prayers and the liturgies found in the *Born of the Spirit* catechetical series used in many Catholic schools across the country. Rather, they are offered as an answer to requests from teachers who find it challenging to pray spontaneously when something happens in the classroom or in the lives of the students.

All prayer is two-pronged: it involves speaking and listening. Praying means being aware of the other's presence; for Christians, this means knowing that God is present to us when we pray.

There are many ways to pray. In times of great sadness or grief, people often find comfort in praying the words of traditional prayers. At other times, people do not even use words to pray; through music or gesture or action, their prayer is embodied and requires no words. We believe that God listens to our prayers no matter what the language or mode. In these prayers for the classroom, the students are encouraged to become the active pray-ers, adding their own words.

Although you may wish to use the words of the prayers as they are, praying in your own words is strongly recommended. You will become more comfortable doing so as you go along. Try following these prayers as models for a while, then start to use your own words. If you teach junior students, ask them to compose their own prayers. This will give them ownership of their class prayer, making these experiences more meaningful for them. Beware of too many words! Sometimes our liturgies, prayers and ritual experiences can be too wordy. When there are too many words, our attention may wander. When it comes to prayers, less is usually more.

When praying with children, especially primary children, here are three key areas to focus on:

• Help them pray in *gratitude*. Thanking God for the people, events and happenings of their lives is more important than asking God for things.

• Teach them to *praise* God for the wonder of creation and for all the gifts of life. Gratitude and praise go hand in hand. Children have a natural sense of awe and are fascinated by the world around them. They often notice things of wonder that adults overlook.

• Remind them to *pray for others*. This is a good way for children to play an active role in the lives of family members, friends, classmates and even people they don't know but have heard about in the news.

As they grow older, they can learn to *ask God's forgiveness* and to *make prayers of petition* more often, all the while remembering to thank God for the many blessings and gifts they receive.

Encouraging the students to be aware of God's presence in silence for even two seconds before praying will help them realize that prayer moments are not like the academic, teaching parts of the school day.

Praying with six-year-olds in Grade 1 is, for the most part, different from praying with 11-year-olds in Grade 6. Adapt the language as needed and let older children compose the prayers of the class. Use more silence with older children, as well. Keeping the ritual constant, though, is just as important with older children as with younger ones: a lit candle, the liturgical colours, the same ritual actions and gathering space, and so on, will help all children to pray well.

Here is a basic method of preparing spoken, spontaneous Christian prayers: *You, Who, Do, Through*. Let's take a closer look at each of these.

YOU: Prayer is only prayer when we address God. (Reading a poem or meditation may lead us to prayer, but in itself is not prayer.) Begin by addressing God with one of the many "conventional" titles for God, and add an adjective to describe God: e.g., *Loving God, Gracious God, God our Creator, God of all seasons.* We can of course call

God "Father," but not to the exclusion of other images or attributes. The Bible uses many images for God, such as God as a mother eagle (Psalm 91/92), God as a parent (Deuteronomy 8:5), and God as rock (Psalm 42). Helping your students to develop a range of images of God can give them a richer understanding of God.

WHO: After addressing God, it is common practice to name an attribute or action of God: e.g., Merciful God, you who have walked with us throughout this school year... or Loving God, you who created us in your image... or Gracious God, you who care for us as a mother hen.... This way of praying hearkens back to the Jewish practice, with which Jesus was familiar, of blessing God before any kind of petition was made. Blessing or thanksgiving is an important stance of the creature toward the Creator. Think of the Eucharistic Prayer from the Mass for an excellent example of this Jewish prayer custom: *Blessed are You, Lord, God of all creation, through your goodness we have this bread to offer, which earth has given and human hands have made.*

DO: This is the most variable part of praying using this formula. The "Do" may be a petition for blessing a meeting, an outing, a new endeavour; for healing for someone who is sick; for comfort for the grieving. So after you have addressed God and remembered something that God has done, ask for something: *Bless us as we travel from this school to learn new things. Be with David's family as they welcome a new baby into their home. Please give healing to Sarah's grandmother who is in hospital.* Sometimes the "do" can instead be an acknowledgment or thanksgiving: *We thank you for this beautiful autumn day.*

THROUGH: As part of our Christian prayer tradition, we believe that Jesus is the primary intermediary for us to God. You will recognize the formula for this "Through" section if you think of the presider's prayers from the Mass: e.g., *We pray in the name of Jesus Christ who lives and reigns with You and the Holy Spirit, one God forever and ever. Amen.* We usually conclude our prayers with a reference to one or more of the Trinity: e.g., *We make our prayer through Jesus Christ our Lord* or *We pray in the name of Jesus the master Teacher* or *We ask this blessing in the name of Jesus, who lives and reigns with you and the Holy Spirit, now and forever. Amen.*

You will not always pray each spontaneous prayer using this formula. It is not fixed and invariable. It is meant only as a guideline, especially when you are called upon to lead students (or, for that matter, adults) in prayer with very little notice. The prayers in this book do not always follow this formula.

Getting Started

Set a prayer routine

All human beings, and children in particular, need and respond well to ritual action. Establish a prayer routine at the beginning of the school year. Children are naturally spiritual and ritual beings. They innately pray and "do" ritual in ways adults cannot. The children have not learned our adult preoccupation with ourselves, with externals, with what is "correct."

Children are wonderfully spontaneous and honest when they pray. They do not care about what others think. Their thoughts and prayers come from their hearts and their experience. We as adults have much to learn from them! For example, children have no difficulty raising their arms to God as they pray. (Most adults are too self-conscious to do this regularly or spontaneously.) So if you light a candle whenever you pray formally with a class, the children will know this as part of the ritual, and when you forget they will surely remind you.

The prayers in this resource are meant to be prayed less formally and more spontaneously. Nevertheless, you can create ritual actions for this kind of prayer. Set a signal for the beginning of a prayer, and the children will recognize it and respond. Signals might include

- folding your hands as you ask the children to be still;
- turning off the classroom light (only if this isn't used for other times);
- gathering in a particular place;
- or singing a brief refrain or acclamation.

If the children are older, let them help determine what would work best for their class.

Allow the children's words, prayers and desires to be spoken freely and without censure. Young children need to be formed in the ways of prayer. As noted earlier, helping them to pray in thanksgiving and praise is the first way to lead them into

13

prayer. Second, helping them to pray for others and other living things (rather than inanimate objects, such as toys) is the way to introduce petition-type prayers. Incorporating time for the children to name their petitions out loud is a key part of classroom prayer for most Catholic teachers. Joined with the prayers of everyone, this classroom prayer becomes the liturgical prayer of the gathered classroom community. The children learn that, no matter what they pray for individually, their prayers are joined to all the others so that the whole class prays as one.

Always incorporate general petitions for the world and the community when you pray together. The children need to exercise their baptismal priesthood by interceding for the life of the world, as the parish community does each time it gathers. Of course the children will have no idea that this is what they are doing, but they will learn about the necessity of praying for others and a world that is bigger than their own. For example, have them pray for children who do not have homes or children who are hungry, or for peace in our world, as well as for the needs of your school or class community.

Your prayer space

While you may pray anywhere in the classroom, you will help the students to be focused and less distracted if you pray in a particular place: e.g., on the rug or near the prayer centre. The space is important: it sets the mood for the prayer that will happen there.

Gesture and body movement

Children can embody their prayer naturally and without inhibition if we guide them. They will pray more easily in the classroom or even at school liturgies if they are invited to make the prayer more than just words. Here are a few ideas:

• Invite them to lift up their arms with palms out when they present a petition.

• Sing a sung refrain. (See the section following on music and prayer for more on this topic.)

• Stand up to pray. (There are contemplative types of prayer that are usually better prayed in a sitting or kneeling posture, but we are not exploring those types of prayer here.)

If petition-type prayers are being prayed, then it is often best to use the same gesture and the same spoken or (even better!) sung response all the time. (You can choose different responses for the liturgical seasons.) It is amazing to pray with children this way and to be moved by the fervency of their prayer. Often in my class we sing the refrain *Ever-loving God, faithful God, hear the prayers of your children* (see *Born of the Spirit* series, years 2, 3 and 6) while we raise our hands towards heaven, palms up, after some children have named aloud their petition or the general petition of the class. Even children who find it hard to stay still are caught up in the holiness of the moment.

Primary children usually benefit from having a ritual prayer position for their hands, such as the "orans" position (upraised arms with palms out) or the hands folded over the heart. Older children ordinarily would not use the folded position, but they will pray with the uplifted hands position if it is presented appropriately to them. You as the teacher know best what works for your class in a given year. As you become more comfortable with prayer gestures, your students will be more comfortable as well.

Silence

Adults are often afraid of silent moments with children. We try to keep them occupied, especially in liturgical services, so they don't talk, fidget or become distracted or distracting. However, we need to believe in their ability to enter into ritual or prayer action precisely because they are children. So, as much as possible, incorporate some silence, even for 10 seconds, into your daily prayer routine. Asking them to pray in the silence of their hearts with eyes closed is one way to encourage children, especially young ones, to focus on their prayer and the prayer of the class community. Your model is the best one when it comes to helping the children to be still and quiet for prayer and to value silence as part of prayer.

Music

If this book were about liturgical prayer in the classroom, it would include a big section on music. But because this book is about spontaneous prayer, the suggested use of music is different. Singing a song or a refrain can be prayer all by itself. To sing, for example, a musical setting of the Glory Be to the Father would be a wonderful way to give praise to God each day. In my classroom, we sing the grace before meals as well as a blessing upon each other at the end of the day. This blessing song becomes the gift to visitors to our class when we wish to thank them.

If the children learn a sung refrain, it can be the response to intercessory prayer or prayers in the litany form. (See the *Ever-loving God* response found in the *Born of the Spirit* series, years 2, 3 and 6, for one example of a sung refrain that the students will easily make their own.) Pair a sung response with an arm gesture and the prayer is immediately embodied and enriched beyond the words-only form.

Another way to incorporate music is to have soft instrumental music playing while the prayer words are being spoken. A particular piece of music may be sung or played as a beginning to all prayer in your classroom. This music serves to help the students change to a prayer mode from whatever activity they have been doing.

You might also consider, especially with primary children, singing the Amen at the end of your prayers. If this is done every time you pray, it will become part of the regular ritual and the children will do it spontaneously without prompting from the teacher.

In the litany prayers, it is always preferable to have the response sung. You may make up the tune for these, if you like, or have someone who is musical help you. Singing a response on one or two notes, in a chant-like fashion, makes it easiest for everyone to learn and sing by heart. Sometimes just listening to a piece of music reverently and quietly can lead the children into their own unspoken prayer with God.

Ways of praying

There are many ways to pray with children in a classroom. For very young primary children, it is often best if the children repeat the words, a few at a time, after the teacher, until the whole prayer is prayed.

For children who can read, the prayer can be printed on chart paper. However, the majority of prayers in this book are meant to be prayed spontaneously, so writing them out defeats the intent. In many instances, a junior student may lead the prayer while reading it from the book. It is important that whoever leads the prayer follows the ritual the class has for praying – gathering in a certain place, making the sign of the cross at the beginning or the end, singing a refrain, and so on. The prayers of the Christian tradition are usually prayed from memory; see Part 3 of this book for these texts. These prayers can be written out for students who can read if they do not yet know them by heart.

If the teacher or another leader begins a prayer, she or he can then invite the rest of the students to respond when appropriate and as indicated in the prayer texts.

Praying *antiphonally* is one way of praying the psalms that religious congregations have used for centuries. In antiphonal prayer, one side or section speaks first, and then the other side or section responds. The prayer is thus prayed back and forth. Most of the prayers in this book do not lend themselves to antiphonal prayer. However, the litanies can be prayed this way or with a leader/response method.

Layout of the book

As you can see from the table of contents, the prayers in this book are sorted by the months of the school year and then followed by particular times calling for prayer. In this way, the liturgical year of the Church is also highlighted. Although some prayers for feast days are in this book, you can find prayers for the other important feast days of the liturgical year in *Prayers for the School Year* (Novalis, 2005) or the Sacramentary. This is especially true when you wish to observe the feast day of your school's namesake.

Making the sign of the cross

In the Eastern and Western Catholic Christian traditions, tracing the sign of the cross on one's body before, and often after, a spoken prayer has long been part of the custom. In fact, the sign of the cross is often the first prayer we learn. It seems important, then, to retain this practice in some way. I suggest that you choose to make the sign of the cross either at the beginning or at the end of the prayer. My preference is to do this at the end, as the words *We make our prayer through...* are being said. Unfortunately, this gesture often gets translated as a signal to be quiet, or is carelessly done. The key, as always, is your modelling, so that the sign of the cross does not become hurried and meaningless.

Praying to Mary

Praying to and with Mary has been a part of the Catholic Christian tradition for centuries. Before Vatican II (before 1962) people often considered October and May as the months in which to pray to Mary. Since Vatican II (through Pope Paul VI's teaching in *Marialus Cultus*), we more correctly highlight Mary during Advent. This keeps the prayer in harmony with the liturgical year and reduces the temptation to separate devotion to Mary from a connection with her Son, Jesus. You will find the three traditional prayers of Mary – the Magnificat, the Angelus and the Hail Mary – in Part 3. Praying any of these with your class during Advent is highly recommended.

Using scripture

Another time-honoured Christian tradition is praying with scripture. Scripture does not tend to lend itself to spontaneous prayer, but some of our traditional prayers are scripture-based (e.g., Hail Mary, Magnificat, Our Father, Glory Be). These can of course always be used in the classroom.

Using scripture quotes in the special liturgical seasons, such as Advent, Lent and Easter, or using a particular biblical story you are studying is easily done. For example, if you are discussing the Prodigal Son during Lent, you might refer to it in a prayer such as the following: *Merciful God, just as you helped the younger son to return to his father, we ask that you help us to recognize our own need to ask forgiveness and to return to you.* Or, when addressing God, you could give an attribute of God related to a biblical story you are exploring: *Loving God, you gave your Son, Jesus, the power to feed 5000 people with only five loaves and two fish. Help us always to trust in your goodness and to recognize you in the people around us.*

Reading a scripture passage and asking the students what it inspires them to pray for is another way to use scripture for prayer.

* * *

May you and your class know the satisfying and comforting presence of God as you pray together throughout the year.

Part 2
Prayers

Prayers for September to June

September

First Day of School

Primary

Loving God, we thank you for gathering us together as this class. We thank you for the summer vacation, which was so much fun. Thank you for our school. Help us to grow together this year into a loving class family. Bless us as we learn and as we play. We pray in the name of Jesus your Son. Amen.

Junior

Gracious God, we gather again for a new school year. We thank you for the summer vacation that has refreshed us. We give you thanks for our school, our teachers, our classmates, and for all that we will learn this year. Bless our days in school. Help us to be good friends to each other. We pray this in the name of Jesus, the master teacher. Amen.

Thanksgiving at the Beginning of the School Year

Primary

At the beginning of this school year, we thank you, God, for so many things: for our school, for desks and books, for pencils and paper, for crayons and paint. We thank you, too, for all the teachers, assistants and parents who help us to learn, and for those who make this school a happy, safe place: the caretakers, the secretary, the volunteers, the priest from _____ parish, the crossing guards, the principal and vice-principal. Help us to appreciate everything that is done for us. In Jesus' name we pray. Amen.

School

Junior

Junior students could compose their own prayer including everything at school for which they are thankful.

"This is the day the Lord has made; let us rejoice and be glad in it" (Psalm 118).

God, your servant David wrote this psalm about you and your creation. Help us always to be thankful for each day and to use it well. We thank you for this day, for the learning and the fun we will have. Bless all of our days. We ask this + [make the sign of the cross here] in the name of the Father, and of the Son and of the Holy Spirit. Amen.

Prayer about Learning

Primary

Dear God, we learned a lot last year. We may have forgotten some things over the summer. We want to learn more new things this year. Bless our teachers and help us to learn all about your world. Please help us to learn…. [*you could ask the children to name things here they would like to learn this year – for example, to read, to do multiplication, to do cursive writing, to write great stories, to learn about space*]. Bless our bodies and minds as we learn. We ask this in the name of Jesus your Son. Amen.

Junior

Holy God, you taught your Son, Jesus, about many things when he was a child. He valued all the lessons he learned from his earthly parents and the elders. As we begin a new school year, we are excited about all the new things we will learn this year. Bless our learning. Bless our parents and teachers who will guide us. May we use the knowledge we gain to help others and to spread your Good News. We ask this in the name of Jesus your Son, the master teacher. Amen.

Prayer for Friends

Primary

Loving God, you are the best friend we can have. We ask today that you help us to be good friends to each other. Help us to be fair, kind and unselfish. Keep our friends safe and happy. Bless us and bless all friends in this community. We pray in the name of Jesus, who was always the friend of children. Amen.

Junior

Gracious God, you are always a faithful friend to each one of us. You watch over us every day. Help us to value our old friends from last year. Help us also to make new friends this year. Especially, we ask that you help us to be good friends: to be kind, caring and unselfish. Bless all friends and teach us to love as your Son Jesus loved his friends. We ask this in his name. Amen.

Traditional Prayers

Ensure that junior students know how to pray these prayers of the Roman Catholic tradition: Our Father, Glory Be, Hail Mary. In September, pray the Glory Be and the Lord's Prayer regularly. (See Part 3 for these and other traditional prayers.)

Grades 2 and 3 students have learned these prayers; review them in September. Grade 1 students are not officially introduced to these prayers until later in the school year in the Born of the Spirit series. Children who regularly attend church or who pray with their families at home may already know the Our Father. Teaching the Glory Be as a way to give God praise and thanks makes eminent sense in September. If you print this prayer on a chart, you can also use it with initial tracking/reading/ phonics instruction.

As well, have students pray a grace before meals each day. See page 70 for a selection of graces.

October

October 4: Feast of St. Francis of Assisi

Primary

Dear God, today is the feast when we remember St. Francis of Assisi, who loved all of nature, and especially animals. St. Francis also prayed for peace in the world. Like St. Francis we, too, ask for peace in our world, especially where people are being hurt or killed. We pray for animals and for our pets (*children could name their pets here if they wish*). We ask that you help us always to care for and respect the creatures you have made. May we be gentle and loving, as St. Francis was. We ask this in Jesus' name. Amen.

Junior: St. Francis' Prayer for Peace*

Lord, make me an instrument of your peace.
Where there is hatred, let me sow love;
Where there is injury, pardon;
Where there is doubt, faith;
Where there is despair, hope;
Where there is darkness, light;
Where there is sadness, joy.
Divine Master, grant that I may not so much seek to be consoled,
    as to console;
to be understood as to understand;
to be loved as to love.
For it is in giving that we receive,
it is in pardoning that we are pardoned,
and it is in dying that we are born to eternal life.

* *Although this prayer was not written by St. Francis, it is attributed to him.*

Thanksgiving

At this time of year, praying using the traditional litany form is a good option. Teacher or a student begins:

Loving God, at this beautiful time of year, when the trees are dressed in wonderful colours and we are enjoying all the fruits and vegetables of the harvest, we thank you… [*now each child can name out loud something or someone for which he or she is thankful; to each thing or person named, the class responds, We give you thanks, O Lord, or something similar. Junior classes could decide upon the class response*]:

For juicy apples

Response (R): We give you thanks, O Lord [*or sing the response with an arm gesture as discussed in Part 1; see Appendix 3 for sources of some sung responses*]

For autumn leaves/R
For my (our) family/R
For grandparents/R
For friends/R
For this school/R
For our country, Canada/R
For people who love us/R
For Jesus, who died for us/R
For God, who created us/R

Praying the litany after a writing exercise when each child has written their own litany is a good approach for junior students (and also could provide for integration and creativity). Primary classes could write their own class litany, which the teacher could record on chart paper. The litanies could be expanded upon each day in the week leading up to the Thanksgiving weekend. The new litany would be prayed each day.

Colours of Fall

God our Creator, you have made our world so beautiful at this time of year. For the red, orange and yellow leaves that adorn the trees, we give you thanks. May we always appreciate the beauty of the world you have created, and may we always take good care of it. We pray in Jesus' name. Amen.

October 31: Halloween

Primary

God, we are so very excited about dressing up for Halloween. Bless our trick-or-treating and keep us safe. Bless the homes we visit and the people who give us treats. Help us also to share the goodies we receive. We pray in Jesus' name, the friend of children. Amen.

Junior

God, we ask your blessing on our trick-or-treating tonight. Watch over us and bless the people whose homes we visit. We ask this in Jesus' name. Amen.

November

November 1: All Saints' Day

Primary

Dear God, today we remember the saints: people who lived the way Jesus taught and who told others about you. Please help us to be kind and to love like Jesus did. Thank you for being patient with us, God. Amen.

Junior

Loving God, today the Church remembers everyone who has given us a model of how to follow Jesus. For all these saints, and for _____ _____(insert here the patron or namesake of your school and an attribute of him or her), we thank you. We also thank you for the saints we find in our own lives: our parents, grandparents, and anyone else who has been a model of faith for us. Help us to live as the saints did and to follow your law of love every day. We pray in Jesus' name. Amen.

See also the Litany of the Saints (in Part 3). Have junior students compile their own list of saints whom they wish to invoke. The usual way of praying this prayer is sung. If students are comfortable doing so, have one student say or sing the saint's name and have the rest of the class respond in song: e.g., St. Michael R/ Pray for us.

Part 3 also contains some prayers written by saints that may inspire prayers in junior students.

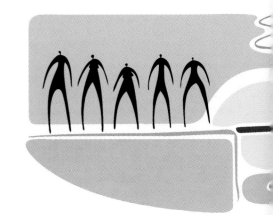

November 2: All Souls' Day

Today the Church remembers everyone who has died.

Primary

God our Father, when someone dies we are very sad. But we know that they go to be with you in heaven. May we always keep alive the memory of the people we have loved in this life. Today, please be with those people who are dying and bring them peace. We ask this in the name of Jesus your Son. Amen.

Junior

God our Father, today is All Souls' Day in our Church, and we remember everyone who has died. We especially remember _____
_____ (*invite students to name people they know who have died*). May we always keep alive the memory of the people we have loved in this life. Today, please be with people who are dying and bring them peace. We ask this in the name of Jesus your Son. Amen.

November 11: Remembrance Day

God of all peace, today we remember the men and women who died in the wars so that our country could be free. These brave people gave their lives for their country and for all the people, including us, who would come after them. For them we thank you. May each of us work for peace in our hearts, in our families and in our country. We ask this through Jesus Christ our Lord. Amen.

Peace Prayer

See October for the Peace Prayer of St. Francis. If you wish, choose a version to sing with your class.

Primary

Holy God, we pray today for peace in our world. Please help the leaders of countries to get along. Please be with the children in places where the adults are fighting and hurting each other. Help us also to be kind and gentle with each other. We ask this in the name of Jesus, who wants everyone to get along. Amen.

Junior

God of all peace, today we pray for peace in our world. We pray, too, for peace here at home and in our communities and families. Help the leaders of countries to work for peace and to make sure that people can live in peace. Bless the peacemakers who work to make peace happen in the war-torn countries of the world. Be with the children in

31

these places who are afraid. Help each one of us to be a peacemaker at home and at school. We make our prayer through Jesus, who came to bring peace. Amen.

Prayer for Our Country

God of all creation, we thank you for our country, Canada. We are so blessed to live in a country where we have freedom, food, lakes, forests and farmland (or have students name here things about Canada for which they are thankful). Bless Canada, its leaders and its people. Help us to take great pride in our country and to keep it a safe and happy place for all. We pray + in the name of the Father and of the Son and of the Holy Spirit. Amen.

December

First Snowfall

Wow, Lord! Thank you so much for the snow and the fun we will have in it. Amen.

Waiting

Primary

Loving God, it is December and Christmas will be here soon. It is so hard to wait because we are so excited. Please help us to be patient just like Mary was when she waited for Jesus to be born. We ask this in Jesus' name. Amen.

Junior

Gracious God, long ago Mary waited patiently for the birth of her Son, Jesus, in Bethlehem. Help us during this month to learn how to wait patiently, too. We pray for all people who are waiting now: for expectant mothers, for loved ones who are away and waiting to come home, for sick people waiting for treatment or waiting to get better, for people waiting to get jobs. We ask all this in the name of Emmanuel, who is to come. Amen.

This is the traditional Advent prayer of waiting for the Messiah. "Maranatha" is an Aramaic word.

Maranatha, come, Lord Jesus, come!

Angelus

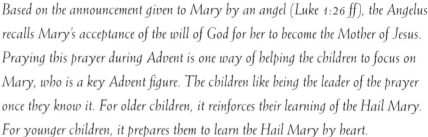

Based on the announcement given to Mary by an angel (Luke 1:26 ff), the Angelus recalls Mary's acceptance of the will of God for her to become the Mother of Jesus. Praying this prayer during Advent is one way of helping the children to focus on Mary, who is a key Advent figure. The children like being the leader of the prayer once they know it. For older children, it reinforces their learning of the Hail Mary. For younger children, it prepares them to learn the Hail Mary by heart.

Ask the children to select an intention for which to pray the Angelus each day during Advent (e.g., for children in the world who need food; for mothers expecting babies; for families without homes). After you have modelled being the leader, let children take turns leading the prayer. It is usually helpful to have the full text on a chart at the beginning. Towards the end of the month, it won't be needed if the Angelus is prayed each day. Doing so at the same time and with the class in the same position or posture will help the children to make the ritual their own.

Leader: The angel of the Lord declared unto Mary

Response by all / And she conceived by the Holy Spirit.

Leader: Hail Mary, full of grace, the Lord is with you. Blessed are you among women and blessed is the fruit of your womb, Jesus.

R/ Holy Mary, Mother of God, pray for us sinners now and at the hour of our death. Amen.

Leader: I am the handmaid of the Lord.

R/ Be it done unto me according to your word.

Hail Mary…

Leader: And the Word was made flesh

R/ and dwelt among us.

Hail Mary…

Leader: Pray for us, O holy Mother of God

R/ That we may be made worthy of the promises of Christ.

All: Pour forth, we beseech you, O Lord, your grace into our hearts, that we, to whom the incarnation of Christ your Son was made known by the message of an angel, may by his passion and death be led to the glory of his resurrection. We ask this through Christ our Lord. Amen.

Leaving for christmas vacation

Holy God, it is time for us to have a break from school. We are excited and ready to spend time with our families and friends. The teachers are, too! Just as Mary and Joseph journeyed to Bethlehem for your Son's birth, many of us will be travelling, too. Keep all of us safe. May we remember, in the midst of gifts and special meals, that it is your Son's birth that we celebrate. Bring us back to school refreshed and ready for another term. We ask this in the name of Jesus, Emmanuel. Amen.

January

Epiphany

This prayer is prayed only if this feast occurs after the return to school from the holidays; it is usually the Sunday after the New Year in the revised liturgical calendar. Many people associate Epiphany specifically with January 6.

Primary

Long ago, God, the three wise men travelled a long way to see the baby Jesus. Then they told the rest of the world about him. May we, like the wise men, tell others about Jesus so they can learn of your great love for all of us. We ask this in the name of Jesus, Emmanuel. Amen.

Junior

Loving God, long ago you showed Jesus to the rest of the world through the eyes of the three kings. As we observe this time of Epiphany, help us also to reveal your Son to those around us by our words and our actions. May our lives and our faith show the world how much you love us. We pray in the name of Jesus, Emmanuel. Amen.

New Year's Resolutions *(Junior)*

Pray this prayer after a discussion and possibly the formulation of New Year's resolutions.

Loving God, continue to walk with us through this new year. As we make decisions to take on new ways and get rid of old, sometimes bad, habits, we ask that you give us the strength to follow through on our resolutions. May we be gentle with ourselves and yet courageous enough to try hard each day to be true to ourselves. We ask this in the name of Jesus, your Son. Amen.

Winter Fun

Primary

Holy God, you have given us the seasons to mark out the year. Now that winter is here, we thank you for all that we can do in this season: (*let the children name activities/sports here*). We love to play in the snow. Be with any children who cannot stay warm in this chilly season and help us always to be thankful for warm clothes, heated homes and food. We pray in Jesus' name. Amen.

Junior

Ask the students to make up a list of winter things for which they are grateful (*e.g., hockey, hot chocolate, skiing, etc.*). This could be interwoven with language arts and science, if desired. Then pray a litany of thanks, such as the following:

For the thrill of skating. / R. We give you thanks.

For hot chocolate, which warms our bodies. / R. We give you thanks.

Winter Storms *(Primary and Junior)*

Dear God, today there is a winter storm outside. While we are warm inside our school, we pray for those people who must work outside and for those who are homeless. We pray for everyone who is travelling and for the workers who clear the roads and highways. Keep everyone safe. We ask this in Jesus' name. Amen.

Winter carnival/Playday *(Primary)*

God of all the seasons, we thank you that we can play outside today. We thank you for the fun we will have with our friends and classmates. We thank you for the older students and teachers who have planned this day for us. Help us always to be polite and fair players on our teams. In Jesus' name we pray. Amen.

Week of Prayer for christian Unity

(Junior)

This week is usually observed near the end of January. Many schools receive packages of materials prepared by local churches. Often you can adapt this material for class prayer services in the Junior grades.

Loving and gracious God, Christian people across the world pray to you and worship you. Sadly, they do not always agree on how to do this. Help everyone who believes in you to be open to the ways of others who are different from themselves. May we try to learn about all Christians so that we can respect their traditions and teach them about ours. We ask this in the name of Jesus Christ, who is the source of our unity and our way to you. Amen.

February

February 2: Groundhog Day *(Primary)*

God of all creation, long ago you made the animals of the forest. Today we observe the tradition of Groundhog Day, when we look ahead to the arrival of spring. Bless all the animals, especially those that hibernate. Help us, too, to get ready to leave winter behind and to welcome the warmth and new life of spring. We ask this in the name of Jesus our brother. Amen.

Ash Wednesday

Before Ash Wednesday, take time to explain to the children what Lent is and how we observe it in the Catholic Christian tradition. Prepare young children in particular for the imposition of ashes on their foreheads and the significance of this action. You can find prayer services and ideas for how to prepare children for Lent in the Canadian Bishops' Born of the Spirit (K to 6) series. Use the prayers below if there is no school liturgy on Ash Wednesday.

Primary

Loving God, today we begin Lent. We are preparing to celebrate Easter, when your Son Jesus rose from the dead. Help us to be kind to each other. May we help others with our prayers and by giving food and money to those who don't have enough. May the cross on our foreheads remind us that Jesus loved us very much. We pray in his name. Amen.

Junior

Gracious God, today we begin the observance of Lent with the placing of ashes on our foreheads. As you watched over Jesus in his forty days in the desert, be with us during these forty days as we prepare to celebrate Easter. May our works of kindness, our prayers and our fasting help us to be ready for the great feast of your Son's resurrection. We pray + (*make the sign of the cross here*) in the name of the Father, and of the Son and of the Holy Spirit. Amen.

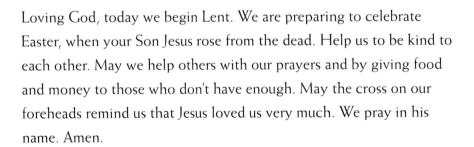

February 14: Valentine's Day

Primary

God of love, we thank you for this fun day of hearts and valentines. We thank you for our friends and classmates. We thank you for our parents, who gave us life. Please help everyone in the world to be more loving. Help us to be kind and loving in this classroom and school too. We ask this + in the name of the Father, and of the Son and of the Holy Spirit (*make the sign of the cross here*). Amen.

Junior

Loving God, we thank you for this special day to focus on love. In our world where there is still unrest and war, we ask that you change the hearts of those who promote hatred and fighting. Help all people to be more loving and kind. May we, too, remember to be kind to each other. May we learn to be more loving every day. In Jesus' name we pray. Amen.

Stations of the cross

This devotion of the Roman Catholic tradition is highly recommended during Lent.
As a class or a division, you might consider gathering during the later weeks of Lent,
and particularly during Holy Week, to pray the Stations as a group. If you cannot
go to a church that has the Stations, set up large pictures or Stations in the gym or
a hallway to help the children pray and move as the Stations are intended. See Part
3, Traditional Prayers, for outlines of the traditional Stations and the scriptural
Stations. There are several adaptations of the Stations available that make them more
accessible for school-age children. In a gym, with lowered lights, music and candles,
the Stations prayer experience can be very powerful for children.

Reconciliation

Lent is traditionally a time of penitence and reconciliation in the Christian tradition. In addition to a communal service of reconciliation, with or without the celebration of the sacrament, consider praying a weekly prayer of forgiveness in your classroom during Lent.

Primary

God our Father, sometimes we are not always as kind as we should be. Sometimes we say and do mean things that hurt people's feelings. Sometimes we think only of ourselves. We ask you to forgive us for these times (*ask the children to think silently of those times recently when they have hurt others*). May we, too, forgive those who have hurt us. We ask this through Jesus, who taught us to be loving and forgiving. Amen.

Junior

Loving and merciful God, we ask you to forgive us for the times we have hurt others; for the times we have been mean or unkind; for the times when we have thought only of ourselves (*ask the students to think silently of times they have been selfish or unkind*). For all these times, we are sorry. We ask you to help us be more loving, as your Son taught us to be. We pray in his name. Amen.

See also the communal prayer for forgiveness in the Prayers for School Life section.

March

March Break

Loving God, you always watch over us when we are in school or away from school. During the next week of holidays, watch over each of us. Help us to stay safe. May we all enjoy our time of relaxation and rest; may we return refreshed for our last term of study this year. Bless our teachers, our principal and everyone who works at our school, too. We ask this in Jesus' name. Amen.

March 17: St. Patrick's Day

Dear God, long ago you sent St. Patrick to teach the people of Ireland about you, your Son and the Holy Spirit. Bless the people of Ireland and help them to live in peace. Bless everyone today who continues St. Patrick's job of telling others about you: our parents, our priests, our teachers and everyone who preaches the gospel. We ask this in Jesus' name. Amen. St. Patrick, pray for us.

March 19: Feast of St. Joseph

Loving God, you chose Joseph to care for Mary and your Son. May we be like Joseph: gentle, caring and responsible. May our country, Canada, which honours Joseph as its patron saint, also be a sign of these values. We pray in the name of Jesus Christ, who lives and reigns with you and the Holy Spirit, one God forever and ever. Amen.

Signs of spring

Lord God, as the winter days get warmer and the promise of spring is in the air, we thank you for all the signs of spring we see (*have the children name some of these signs here*). Thank you for the new life and new plants that will arrive in the next few weeks. Thank you for the returning birds. Thank you for the green grass, which is starting to show after all these months of snow and cold. May we always appreciate the beauty of this world. We pray in Jesus' name. Amen.

April

Easter

Primary

Option: Sing an Alleluia refrain to begin.

Dear God, Jesus rose from the dead a long time ago. Thank you for this gift of Jesus that we celebrate year after year. Thank you also for the new life that Easter gives us. Help us always to be children of the light who sing Alleluia to you and Jesus. We pray in Jesus' name. Amen.

Junior

Option: Sing an Alleluia refrain to begin.

Jesus is risen and Alleluia is our song! At this happy Easter time, Lord, we give you thanks for so many things. We thank you for raising Jesus from the dead. We thank you also for the freedom this gives us to be forgiven. We thank you for this season of fifty days when we celebrate Jesus' resurrection. May we always be an Easter people and may we always sing Alleluia to praise your name. We pray in the name of the risen Lord, Jesus Christ. Amen.

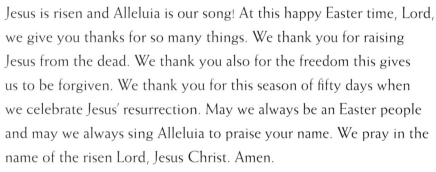

Spring*

Creator God, we give you thanks for this wonderful season of spring! Thank you for the green grass, the new buds on the trees, the baby animals being born and the flowers that are starting to sprout. Thank you for the rain and sun that help these plants to grow. May we take good care of this earth you have given us, and may we grow in you as we try each day to be more like Jesus. We ask this in his name. Amen.

* See March for an early spring prayer.

A Rainy Day

God, it is raining and we have to stay inside today. Thank you for the rain, which helps the plants to grow. Thank you for the new life we see all around us. Help us to remember how important the rain is when we are tired of being inside. We ask this in Jesus' name. Amen.

Birds Returning

God, the air is filled with the sight and sounds of the birds returning to their homes after the cold winter. Thank you for the birds, for their beauty and their songs! May they find safe places for their nests. We ask this in the name of Jesus your Son, who was the friend of animals and all creation. Amen.

May

Mother's Day

Primary

Dear God, thank you for our mothers, who take care of us and love us, even when we do unkind things or don't listen. Jesus loved his mother, Mary; help us to be loving children to our moms. We ask this in Jesus' name. Amen.

Junior

Loving God, on Sunday we will honour our mothers. We thank you for all that our mothers do for us. (*Students can name things here if they wish.*) We thank you especially for our mothers' love, which is always there for us. Jesus cared for and loved his own mother, Mary; we ask you to help us always to appreciate and love our mothers. Bless now and always our mothers, our grandmothers and all those who love children like a mother. We ask this in the name of Jesus. Amen.

Pentecost

See Part 3, Traditional Prayers, for the Come, Holy Spirit prayer. This is a good prayer for Primary and Junior students, as it is or added on to the end of another prayer text. (See also the Year 3 In the Spirit We Belong *child's book, from the CCCB* Born of the Spirit *series.)*

Primary

Loving God, you sent Jesus to tell us how much you love us. You sent the Holy Spirit to help us each day. Remind us to ask for the Spirit's help. We ask this in Jesus' name. Amen.

Junior

Gracious God, it is the time of year when we remember that through Jesus you sent the Holy Spirit to help us. Thank you for this Spirit of love. Help us to remember to call upon your Spirit to guide and help us each day, especially when we are confused or sad or when we don't know what to do. Like Jesus, may we know the Spirit's presence in our lives. We ask this in the name of Jesus, your Son, who lives and reigns with you and the Holy Spirit now and forever. Amen.

Spring Flowers

Lord our God, the earth is full of new growth and beautiful flowers. We thank you for springtime and the beauty all around us. We thank you for the flowers, the trees with their new buds and the grass that is getting greener every day. How blessed we are to live on your precious earth! Thank you, God, for this gift of springtime. We pray in Jesus' name. Amen.

June

Father's Day

God our Father, this weekend we will celebrate Father's Day. You gave Jesus an earthly father, Joseph, who cared for him when he was a child. We thank you for our fathers and grandfathers who care for us. We ask you to bless all fathers and all who take the place of fathers in caring for children. We pray this in Jesus' name. Amen.

Track-and-field Meet

Bless us this day, Lord, as we compete in the track-and-field meet. Thank you for the gift of our bodies and all they can do. May we be strong, do our best and have fun. Help us to be good sports and to treat everyone with respect. We ask this in Jesus' name. Amen.

End of the School Year

Dear God, at the end of this school year we are so thankful for all the good things that have happened to us and our class this year (*students can name things here*). We thank you for all we have learned. We thank you for our teachers and parents who have taught us. We thank you for all the new friends we have made and for all the fun things we have done together. Bless us and our teachers as we leave school for the summer holidays. Help us to return in September rested and ready for another new school year. We ask this in the name of Jesus Christ, the master teacher. Amen.

Summer

Loving God, once again the days are long and warm. We look forward to all the fun things that summer offers: swimming, cottages, camp, travel to new places, and playing with friends. Thank you for the seasons and especially for the wonderful days of summer. We pray this in Jesus' name. Amen.

Prayers for Times of Sadness

Death of a Family Member

Primary

Loving God, we are very sad today. _____(*name the person here and the relationship to the class member*) has died. Please be with _____'s family at this time when they are missing their _____ so much. Help them to find comfort from friends and family. We pray for _____ and for his/her family. May we be good friends to _____ when he/she returns to school. We ask this in the name of Jesus, who was also sad when his friend Lazarus died. Amen.

Junior

Loving God, we are very sad today. _____(*name the person here and the relationship to the class member*) has died. Please be with _____'s family at this time when they are missing their _____ so much. Help them to find comfort from friends and family. We pray for _____ and for his/her family. We ask this in the name of Jesus, who cried when his friend Lazarus died. Amen.

(*If appropriate here, and probably only for a Junior class, pray the Eternal Rest prayer for the deceased person. See Part 3: Traditional Prayers.*)

Death of a Pet *(Primary)*

Today, Lord God, we found out that _____'s _____ ___ has died and _____ is very sad. We know that you love animals and we ask that you help_____ remember all the good times he/she enjoyed with his/her pet. Bless veterinarians and everyone who cares for animals. May we provide comfort to our friend who is missing her/his pet so much right now. In Jesus' name we pray. Amen.

Student/ Parent/ Teacher Who is Sick

Gracious God, _____ is sick right now. We pray for
_____ and ask that she/he get better quickly and be
able to return to us (*or to their family, if it is a parent*). Bless all nurses,
doctors and everyone who cares for people who are ill. May all sick
people find comfort through their families and friends. We ask this in
the name of Jesus, who healed many people. Amen.

Family Who is Moving Away

Dear God, our classroom family/community is losing a member and
we are sad. Please bless _____, who is moving away
to a new community and school. May he/she find some new friends
there. May we always be grateful for the time we have spent together
here at _____. (*Ask all the children to raise both arms
towards the student who is moving away.*) We ask that you bless _____
_____ with health, happiness and good friends in _____
_____, + in the name of the Father, and of the Son and of
the Holy Spirit. Amen.

Family experiencing Separation/ Divorce

Primary

Dear God, _____is sad because her/his parents have decided not to live together anymore. Please help _____ _____ to understand and to be free of pain. May we be good friends to her/him. We ask this in Jesus' name. Amen.

Junior

Holy God, you gave us families to love and support us and to help us to grow. When a family cannot continue being together, we know that they are sad. Please be with _____'s family as they start a new life apart from each other. Help each family member to understand, as best they can, what has happened. If there is pain and anger, please help these things to be eased through the caring and love of others. May _____ always find in us a safe place to talk about his/her feelings. May _____ always know that he/she is loved. We ask this in Jesus' name, Amen.

impending Surgery

Gentle God, you have healed so many people. Tomorrow _____ _____ will be having an operation at the hospital. Please guide the doctors and nurses so that the surgery may be successful and so that _____ may return to us soon. Keep _____ _____ in your loving care. We pray this in Jesus' name. Amen.

Prayer for Parents Who Work Away from the Family

Loving God, in _____'s family, his/her father/mother must work away from this community. Please watch over all parents who are separated from their families. Keep them happy and help them to return home safely whenever they travel. We ask this + in the name of the Father and of the Son and of the Holy Spirit. Amen.

Prayers for Joyful Times

A New Baby in a Student's Family

God of creation, today we are so excited! A new baby boy/girl has been born to _____'s family. We thank you for this new life and for the happiness she/he brings to _____'s family. Bless all the family members as they welcome this gift of love into their family. We ask this in the name of Jesus. Amen.

Birthday

Loving God, today we thank you for _____, who
is celebrating a birthday. We ask that you bless _____
with a fun day and happy days in the year ahead. Keep _____
_____ always close to you. We ask this in Jesus' name. Amen.

Birthday Blessing

Ask the students to extend one arm towards the birthday person while the following is spoken or led by the teacher:

May God, who gave you life, bless you. (*All answer, Amen.*)
May God walk with you throughout the coming year./Amen.
May God keep you safe and give you peace./Amen.

Accomplishment by an individual or by a Group/Team

God, you give us our bodies and brains as gifts. Today we are grateful that _____ has used these gifts to _____ _____. We are happy and we thank you that _____ _____ was/were able to accomplish this. We take delight in this accomplishment/prize and we praise you for _____. Bless all who (*add here whatever was done: e.g., run, do public speaking, play*) and continue to bless _____. We pray + in the name of the Father, and of the Son and of the Holy Spirit. Amen.

Prayers for School Life

Daily Morning Prayer

Primary

Dear God, we thank you for this day. We thank you for our families and friends. We thank you for our classmates. Be with us as we work and play today. Help us always to be kind to each other. We pray + in the name of the Father, and of the Son and of the Holy Spirit. Amen.

Junior

During the first few days of school, brainstorm with the students about what they would like to include in a daily morning prayer. Guide the discussion by suggesting that they thank God for the day and ask a blessing on themselves and their activities each day. Once the text has been composed, display it prominently in the classroom. Pray it in different ways: have a student pray it in the name of the whole class; have the whole class pray it together, beginning or ending with the sign of the cross; have children express particular needs or petitions before the class prays the prayer. If the school is named after a saint, the class could decide to add "St. _____, pray for us" at the end of the prayer before they make the sign of the cross.

Going on a Field Trip

Lord our God, be with us today on our field trip. Keep us from all harm and help us to remember all the new things we learn. We pray in Jesus' name. Amen.

Asking for Forgiveness

Today, God, we are not very proud of ourselves. We have not thought of others first and we have _____
(*students can insert what they wish here after a discussion with the teacher*). Help us to change our ways and to be kind to those around us. Help us to ask forgiveness and to forgive others. In Jesus' name we pray. Amen.

Prayer at the End of a School Day

Primary

God, we thank you for this day. Watch over us tonight and help us return safely tomorrow. We ask this in Jesus' name. Amen.

Junior

Ask the students during the first week of school to compose a class prayer for the year. Discuss with them what they wish to ask God to do for them each evening and for what they might be grateful each day. Pray your class prayer together before the final bell rings.

Aaronic Blessing *(Junior)*

May the Lord bless you (us) and keep you (us).

May the Lord make his face to shine upon you (us) and be kind (gracious) to you (us).

May the Lord lift up his countenance upon you (us) and grant you (us) peace.

Prayer before Meals

You can choose from many texts for grace before meals. Here are several possibilities (the first one is the traditional one). Or, invite the children to compose their own grace before meals.

+ Bless us, O Lord, and these your (thy) gifts,
which we are about to receive from your (thy) bounty (goodness),
through Christ our Lord. Amen.

 + For food in a world where many walk in hunger,
for friends in a world where many walk alone,
for faith in a world where many walk in fear,
we give you thanks, O God.
(*The World Hunger Prayer*)

+ God is great, God is good,
let us thank God for our food. Amen.

Singing grace is very suitable especially for Primary children.

• Johnny Appleseed
• For thy gracious blessing
• For health and strength and daily food

Be present at our table, Lord,
Be here and everywhere adored.
Thy creatures bless and grant that we
may feast in paradise with thee.

Report cards

God, you love us very much and you have created each of us to be different. Today when we take our reports cards home, help us to remember that we each have different gifts. Thank you for creating us and for making each of us unique. We ask this in the name of Jesus our brother. Amen.

100th Day in Kindergarten or Grade 1

God, we are amazed that we have already been in school for 100 days this year! Thank you for all we have learned. Thank you for our friends and classmates. Thank you for our teachers and parents, who have taught us all these days. For each and every day we give you thanks and praise. In Jesus' name. Amen.

A Special Day in our School

God our Father, today we observe/celebrate _____
_____ in our school. We thank you for this great opportunity. Bless all
our activities and fun. (*If appropriate*) Bless our visitors. Be with us this
day. We ask this + in the name of the Father, and of the Son and of
the Holy Spirit. Amen.

For children who have celebrated first sacraments

(Reconciliation, First Communion, Confirmation)

Holy God, the children in Grade _____ have recently celebrated
_____. We are happy that they have come to know
you in this special way. Bless them and their parents. Keep them
always close to you. We ask this in Jesus' name. Amen.

Graduation *(Junior)*

Loving God, you have walked with us throughout this school year.
We thank you for your presence and help. Now, at graduation, when
we celebrate all that we have learned, and as we prepare to leave this
school community, we again ask that you be with us on this journey.
Bless our teachers and parents. Bless us with courage as we face the
challenges of a new school and year. Keep us always close to you. We
ask this in the name of Jesus our brother. Amen.

Prayers for anytime

These short prayers can be prayed any time throughout the day.

Thanks be to God.

Alleluia!

Lord, have mercy.

God bless you.

Come, Lord Jesus.

Come, Holy Spirit.

Glory to God in the highest.

Stay with us, Lord.

Part 3
Prayers of the Christian Tradition

Lord's Prayer I

Our Father, who art in heaven,
hallowed be thy name;
thy kingdom come;
thy will be done on earth as it is in heaven.
Give us this day our daily bread;
and forgive us our trespasses
as we forgive those who trespass against us;
and lead us not into temptation,
but deliver us from evil. Amen.

Lord's Prayer II

Our Father in heaven,
hallowed be your name,
your kingdom come, your will be done,
on earth as in heaven.
Give us today our daily bread.
Forgive us our sins
as we forgive those who sin against us.
Save us from the time of trial
and deliver us from evil.
For the kingdom, the power
and the glory are yours,
now and forever. Amen.

© English Language Liturgical Consultation

Glory Be

Glory to the Father,
and to the Son,
and to the Holy Spirit.
As it was in the beginning,
is now, and will be forever. Amen.

Hail Mary

Hail Mary, full of grace,
the Lord is with you.
Blessed are you among women
and blessed is the fruit of your womb, Jesus.
Holy Mary, Mother of God,
pray for us sinners,
now and at the hour of our death. Amen.

Angelus

The angel of the Lord declared unto Mary, and she conceived of the Holy Spirit.
Hail Mary…
Behold, the handmaid of the Lord; be it done to me according to your word.
Hail Mary…
And the word was made flesh, and dwelt among us.
Hail Mary…
Pray for us, O holy Mother of God; that we may be made worthy of the promises
of Christ.
Pour forth, we beseech you, O Lord, your grace into our hearts that we, to whom
the incarnation of your Son was made known by the message of an angel, may
by his passion and cross be brought to the glory of his resurrection. We ask this
through the same Christ, our Lord. Amen.

(For an updated version, see *Blessings and Prayers for Home and Family*, CCCB, 2004.)

Magnificat (Luke 1:46-55)

My soul magnifies the Lord,
and my spirit rejoices in God my Saviour,
for he has looked with favour on the lowliness of his servant.
Surely, from now on all generations will call me blessed;
for the Mighty One has done great things for me,
and holy is his name.
His mercy is for those who fear him
from generation to generation.
He has shown strength with his arm;
he has scattered the proud in the thoughts of their hearts.
He has brought down the powerful from their thrones,
and lifted up the lowly;
he has filled the hungry with good things,
and sent the rich away empty.
He has helped his servant Israel,
in remembrance of his mercy,
according to the promise he made to our ancestors,
to Abraham and to his descendants forever.

Come, Holy Spirit

Come, Holy Spirit,
fill the hearts of your faithful
and kindle in them the fire of your love.
Send forth your Spirit, O Lord,
and renew the face of the earth.

Prayer when someone dies

Eternal rest grant unto him/her, O Lord,
and let perpetual light shine upon him/her.
May he/she rest in peace. Amen.

Quotes from Saints that may inspire prayer (Junior)

St. Francis' peace prayer (attributed to St. Francis)

Lord, make me an instrument of your peace.
Where there is hatred, let me sow love;
Where there is injury, pardon;
Where there is doubt, faith;
Where there is despair, hope;
Where there is darkness, light.
Where there is sadness, joy.
Divine Master, grant that I may not so much seek to be consoled, as to console;
to be understood as to understand;
to be loved as to love.
For it is in giving that we receive;
It is in pardoning that we are pardoned;
And it is in dying that we are born to eternal life.

St. Augustine's prayer

You have made us, O Lord, for yourself
and our hearts are restless until they rest in you. Amen.

Prayer of St. Patrick

May the strength of God pilot us.
    May the power of God preserve us.
May the wisdom of God instruct us.
    May the hand of God protect us.
May the way of God direct us.
    May the shield of God defend us. Amen.

St. Clare of Assisi

Blessed are you, my Lord God, for creating me and giving me life;
and by your death on the cross, blessed are you Jesus for redeeming me
and giving me eternal life. Amen.

Stations of the Cross

Traditional

1. Jesus is condemned to death
2. Jesus takes up his Cross
3. Jesus falls for the first time
4. Jesus meets his Mother
5. Simon of Cyrene helps Jesus to carry his Cross
6. Veronica wipes the face of Jesus
7. Jesus falls for the second time
8. Jesus speaks to the women of Jerusalem
9. Jesus falls for the third time
10. Jesus is stripped and offered vinegar and gall to drink
11. Jesus is nailed to the Cross
12. Jesus dies on the Cross
13. Jesus is taken down from the Cross and given to his Mother
14. Jesus is laid in the tomb

Scriptural

1. The Last Supper
2. In the Garden of Gethsemane
3. Before the Sanhedrin
4. Before Pontius Pilate
5. The whipping and crowning with thorns
6. The carrying of the cross
7. Simon of Cyrene
8. The women of Jerusalem
9. The stripping and crucifixion
10. The second thief
11. Mary and John
12. Death on the cross
13. The new sepulchre
14. The resurrection

Litany of the Saints

Holy Mary, Mother of God. **Pray for us.**
Saint Michael
Holy angels of God
Abraham, Moses and Elijah
Saint Joachim and Saint Anne
Saint Joseph
Saint John the Baptist
Saint Peter and Saint Paul
Saint Andrew
Saint John
Saint Mary Magdalene
Saint Stephen
Saint Ignatius
Saint Lawrence
Saint John de Brébeuf and the holy Canadian Martyrs
Saint Perpetua and Saint Felicity
Saint Agnes
Saint Gregory
Saint Augustine
Saint Athanasius
Saint Basil
Saint Catherine of Siena
Saint Teresa of Avila
Saint Martin
Blessed François de Laval
Saint Benedict
Saint Francis and Saint Dominic
Saint Francis Xavier
Saint John Vianney
Saint Marguerite Bourgeoys
Saint Marguerite d'Youville
Saint Monica
Saint Louis
Blessed Kateri Tekakwitha
(other saints)
All holy men and women

From the Sacramentary (Roman Missal)

The Rosary

In the Rosary, we focus on 20 events or mysteries in the life and death of Jesus.

• Begin the Rosary at the crucifix by praying the *Apostles' Creed*.

• At each large bead, pray the *Our Father*.

• At each small bead, pray the *Hail Mary*.

• At the first three beads it is customary to pray a *Hail Mary* for each of the gifts of faith, hope and love.

• For each mystery, begin with the *Our Father*, recite the *Hail Mary* ten times, and end with *Glory Be*.

The Five Joyful Mysteries:
> The Annunciation (Luke 1:26-38)
>
> The Visitation (Luke 1:39-56)
>
> The Nativity (Luke 2:1-20)
>
> The Presentation (Luke 2:22-38)
>
> The Finding in the Temple (Luke 2:41-52)

The Five Luminous Mysteries:
> The Baptism in the Jordan (Matthew 3:13-17)
>
> The Wedding at Cana (John 2:1-12)
>
> The Proclamation of the Kingdom (Mark 1:15)
>
> The Transfiguration (Luke 9:28-36)
>
> The First Eucharist (Matthew 26:26-29)

The Five Sorrowful Mysteries:
> The Agony in the Garden (Matthew 26:36-56)
>
> The Scourging at the Pillar (Matthew 27:20-26)
>
> The Crowning with Thorns (Matthew 27:27-30)
>
> The Carrying of the Cross (Matthew 27:31-33)
>
> The Crucifixion (Matthew 27:34-60)

The Five Glorious Mysteries:
> The Resurrection (John 20:1-18)
>
> The Ascension (Acts 1:9-11)
>
> The Descent of the Holy Spirit (John 20:19-23)
>
> The Assumption of Mary (John 11:26)
>
> The Crowning of Mary (Philippians 2:1-11)

Appendix 1

The Liturgical Year

September to the end of November is *Ordinary Time* in the church calendar; green is the appropriate colour.

December, for four weeks, is *Advent*; a royal purple is the colour. Advent is now a season of joyful anticipation and not one of penitence. If possible, the purple colour should be a different hue from the one used during Lent. The first Sunday of Advent is the beginning of the liturgical year for the Church. It usually falls on the last Sunday of November.

December 25 until the feast of the Baptism of the Lord is the *Christmas* season; its liturgical colour is white. Often the school break ends before the Christmas season is over. The Baptism of the Lord is usually the Sunday after Epiphany. In the Western Catholic Church, Epiphany is no longer always celebrated on January 6; instead, we celebrate it on the Sunday closest to January 6.

January to mid-February or early March is again *Ordinary Time* (liturgical colour: green) in the church calendar.

Ash Wednesday denotes the beginning of *Lent*. This date changes every year according to the date of Easter. The liturgical colour for Lent is purple. Lent lasts for 40 days (excluding Sundays). The last week of Lent is Holy Week.

Easter begins after the celebration of the Triduum [TRID-oo-um] – Holy Thursday evening until Easter Sunday evening – and lasts for 50 days. The liturgical colour is white. Easter usually extends into early May of the school year, ending with the feast of Pentecost.

May–June is again *Ordinary Time* (green) in the Church's liturgical year.

Appendix 2

Other Helpful Resources

Margaret Bick, *Preparing to Celebrate in Schools*. Ottawa: Novalis, 1997.

Blessings and Prayers for Home and Family. CCCB. Ottawa, 2004.

Children's Daily Prayer (Annual – Intermediate / Senior). Chicago: Liturgical Training Publications.

Rosanna Golino, *Prayers for the School Year*. Ottawa: Novalis, 2005.

Lectionary: Sundays and Solemnities. CCCB: Ottawa, 1992.

Lectionary: Weekdays. CCCB: Ottawa, 1992.

Living with Christ Sunday Missal for Young Catholics (Annual). Ottawa: Novalis.

Sacramentary: The Roman Missal. CCCB.

Gerard Whitty, *Preparing to Celebrate with Children*. Ottawa: Novalis, 1997.

Appendix 3

Music Resources

Catholic Book of Worship III. Ottawa: Canadian Conference of Catholic Bishops, 1994.

Born of the Spirit Catechetical Series. Ottawa: Canadian Conference of Catholic Bishops.

- Year 2: *We Belong to the Lord Jesus*
- Year 3: *In the Spirit We Belong*
- Year 6: *You Shall Be My Witnesses*

Rise Up and Sing. Oregon Catholic Press. Portland, Oregon, 1992 (with CDs).

Music for Children's Liturgy of the Word. Cycles A, B, C. Christopher Walker. Oregon Catholic Press, Portland, Oregon, 1990 (includes cassettes).

Other books of interest

Prayers for the School Year

An indispensable resource for Catholic elementary and secondary schools written by an experienced teacher and consultant. Presents readings and NRSV lectionary–based prayers for each day of the school year, including feast days and following the liturgical seasons. A wonderful addition to your school day! (Prepared according the Canadian Conference of Catholic Bishops' Weekday Lectionary and the Liturgical Calendar.)

Theology for Teachers

A thoughtful, engaging introduction to theology. Readers will enjoy and benefit from the author's down-to-earth relating of theology to faith life. (Suited to the curriculum guidelines of the Institute for Catholic Education for courses in religious education.)

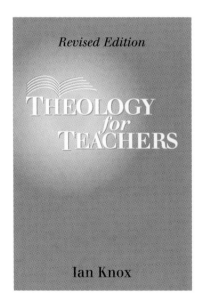

Living with Christ Sunday Missal for Young Catholics

A *fully illustrated Sunday missal* designed to help young Catholics get to know Jesus better, learn about their faith and participate at Mass. Includes all scripture readings for Sundays and feast days (NRSV lectionary). Approved by the Canadian bishops. An ideal gift for children celebrating First Communion or Confirmation.

To find out more about Novalis books, please visit our website:

www.novalis.ca

NOVALIS

Heather Reid was for twelve years the consultant in Religious Education and Family Life Education for the Ottawa-Carleton Catholic School Board. She now happily teaches Grade 1 at Monsignor Paul Baxter School in Nepean. She holds a Master's degree in Liturgy from the University of Notre Dame in Indiana.